The Private Rental Sector

in Germany

OECD Research on private rental sector

Consultancy report: Germany

Author: Prof. Dr.rer.pol. Stefan Kofner, MCIH

Disclaimer: This report does not necessarily represent the official views of the OECD or of the governments of its member countries.

Table of contents

1   **The Private Rental Sector in Germany:**
       Essential research findings and suggestions 5

     1.1   The importance of the Private Rental Sector *5*

     1.2   Tenure neutrality *6*

     1.3   The effectiveness of rental regulation *7*

     1.4   Incentives for new residential construction *11*

     1.5   The role of social housing *13*

2   **Definition of the PRS** **15**

3   **Structure of the housing market** **17**

     3.1   Stock composition *17*

     3.2   Tenant profiles *20*

     3.3   Housing costs for tenants in the PRS *20*

     3.4   Turnover rates *22*

4   **Policies and reforms that impact the PRS** **23**

     4.1   Driving forces and winners / losers of housing reform *23*

     4.2   How rents are set *26*

        4.2.1   Local reference rent and Mietspiegel 27

        4.2.2   Rent caps 29

        4.2.3   Apportionment of modernization costs 30

        4.2.4   Stepped rent 31

        4.2.5   Index-linked rent 32

        4.2.6   Enforcement of the rent controls 33

        4.2.7   Assessment of the impact of the rent controls 34

     4.3   Dismissal protection *38*

        4.3.1   Termination without notice 38

        4.3.2   Dismissal with due notice 38

		4.3.3	Contradiction of the tenant (§§ 574-574b)	39
		4.3.4	Eviction procedures	40
		4.3.5	Assessment of the impact of dismissal protection	41

4.4   *Taxation of rental income* *42*

4.5   *Homeownership subsidies* *44*

4.6   *Housing allowances* *48*

4.7   *Reforms effects on the housing market* *49*

5   **Barriers to a well-functioning housing market and PRS** **51**

5.1   *Supply side barriers* *51*

5.2   *Appropriateness of yields in the PRS* *52*

5.3   *Subsidization of social housing* *53*

5.4   *Lock-in effects/barriers for mobility of social tenants* *56*

5.5   *Flexibility of conversion from other tenures* *57*

6   **Sources** **59**

7   **Annex: Homeownership rates in Germany** **63**

1 The Private Rental Sector in Germany: Essential research findings and suggestions

In a nutshell the German housing system is characterized by

- relative tenure neutrality and no strong fiscal support of owner-occupied housing.
- building up of a large rental housing stock through extensive housing subsidies and generous tax treatment in the past (although these subsidies have been reduced recently).
- a system of temporary subsidies for social housing at moderate profits which finally returns the dwellings to the private market.
- strong tenancy security for decades, which makes that rental housing is regarded as a stable and reliable tenure, almost as secure as owner-occupied housing.
- rent regulation that does not set too strict boundaries on the yields of landlords (although the market rent could be followed more closely).
- a severe market split that has become visible in recent years between ongoing and new tenancies in urban growth regions.

1.1 The importance of the Private Rental Sector

In short, it can be said that the German housing market system is balanced, and that the private rental sector (PRS) is not hampered by many institutional barriers. There is no doubt that the German PRS is a key pillar of the system of housing supply in Germany. According to the German experiences after World War II one precondition for a well-developed rental sector is a combination of protective regulation (i.e. dismissal protection and rent control) and tax incentives for new construction of rental housing. The other is a good state of maintenance and modernization of the existing rental housing stock. A well maintained rental housing stock prevents some richer and more sophisticated households from buying a home of their own. More importantly, it prevents the emergence of prejudice against renting as a tenure. The tax treatment of the capital expenditure in the rental housing stock has always been generous in Germany. The capacity to raise rents in line with modernization costs is a further element of the incentive system to maintain and improve residential buildings.

The German PRS is dominated by small private landlords. The most important factor that can explain why it is mainly small private landlords that are invested in the German market is the tax treatment in the past. Decreasing balance depreciation, directly-deductible maintenance costs and the possibility to deduct resulting losses from the income tax base (negative gearing) in combination with the prospect of tax-free capital gains were especially attractive for well-off private investors with a high personal tax rate.

Institutional landlords play only a minor role. This may offer a starting point to increase the market share of the PRS even further. The most important barriers are presumably in the field of investment legislation. However, in general the supply side structure of the German housing market seems well-balanced. In large parts of the country, there is an effective and only slightly distorted choice between tenures and landlord groups (i.e. public and private landlords as well as cooperatives). There is also an effective competition between tenures and landlord groups.

1.2   Tenure neutrality

The prospects for the German PRS are surely not hampered by all-too-generous subsidies for other housing tenures. Social housing is in constant descent. Each year far more social dwellings lose their status than new social dwellings are constructed. Public housing is in constant descent, too. This is in part due to the privatizations of whole public housing companies. Also the development activities of public housing providers are hampered by financial restrictions, i.e. access to equity capital.

The subsidies for homeownership are on a low level in historical comparison. The "Eigenheimzulage" was cancelled in 2006 already. In personal income taxation the own house is treated as a consumption good. This also applies in case of a sale of an owner-occupied home where no capital gains taxation is applied. Currently, the most important instrument of subsidization is a personal pension scheme known as the "Riester pension".

It is commendable that the German system respects the neutrality of tenures by and large, and prefers owner-occupied housing only to a slight degree, if at all. Particularly in view of the real estate transfer tax constantly screwed by the states[1], further raising the homeownership rate would constitute a major obstacle to the mobility of the labor force. A further increase in the rate of homeownership in the sense of a political objective should therefore be accompanied by a substantial lowering of transaction costs. In principle, there is sufficient leeway for an increase in the rate of homeownership in Germany, without this being necessarily associated with greater risks to the stability of the financial system. Anyway, the transaction costs of acquiring homeownership should be limited, if not reduced.

1.3 The effectiveness of rental regulation

An important question is whether the German PRS is regulated effectively. It is a good thing, that almost all rental agreements are concluded for an indefinite time. The tenants thereby remain flexible and that in turn promotes labor market mobility. To preserve the flexibility of the tenants, however, the possibility of a contractual termination exclusion should be legally barred.

Given the intensity of dismissal protection in Germany renting offers a long-term perspective. Not least this long-term perspective has allowed the rental sector to reach its current size. A lower level of dismissal protection would probably not have much impact in terms of promoting mobility in the long run, because many rental households would then migrate into the owner-occupied sector. This results in the conclusion that one should not create additional barriers to mobility in both sectors by regulation or taxation. This relates to the transaction costs of homeownership as well as to the rental price laws.

---

[1] According to § 11 Grunderwerbsteuergesetz (property transfer tax law), the tax rate is 3.5 per cent. Since 1 September 2006 the federal states may set the tax rate themselves and they have done so extensively. From 1 January 2014 the tax is 6,5 per cent in Schleswig-Holstein and 6 per cent in Berlin. The bulk of the states currently charges 5 per cent.

In general, a simplification of the German rental price laws is recommended in order to increase transparency. The system suffers from excessive complexity. The complexity of the rules and their exceptions combined with the heterogenity in their local application (which has just recently been further increased) tend to make a rational housing policy almost impossible since there is no way to predict the consequences of measures taken. All in all, such a complicated, heterogenous and thus poorly understood system is not very efficient for its stakeholders, i.e. tenants, landlords, courts, administrators and policy-makers.

Particularly striking is the complexity of the German rules for rent price formation. There are huge local differences in the practical application of the rules for the determination of the local reference rent (abbreviated "LRR" in the following, see below, 4.2.1 and 4.2.7).

A standardization and simplification of the local reference rent system is recommended. The stepped rent could be abolished as a means of legislative simplification. Also, to be effective, it needs to be accompanied by a long-term exclusion of the tenant's right to terminate the lease agreement with due notice. This undesirably affects labor market mobility.

As for the index-linked rent, the reasons for its low proliferation should be investigated. In addition, it should be considered to allow for the combination of the index-linked rent with modernization-related rent increases.

Furthermore, it should be considered to make Mietspiegel obligatory in cities with a population above a certain minimum level. In addition, binding rules should be introduced for their preparation that leave enough leeway for the consideration of local peculiarities such as necessary sample size and stock composition. Also, the Mietspiegel should be updated mandatory every two years.

In small cities without a Mietspiegel, the LRR should be replaced by a simple adjustment rule in the form of a claim of the landlord to compensate for his loss of purchasing power, plus a slight markup.

Rules linked to the scarcity situation of individual markets (like the new 10 per cent rent cap for new leases adopted by the coalition partners or the lower rent caps for ongoing contracts already in force in some cities, see below, 4.2.2) should generally be avoided. Such rules provide for uncertainty of investors, lack of transparency and increased administration and litigation costs. The complexity of the system of rent price formation cannot be increased indefinitely.

The modernization apportionment should be maintained however, because it is an important part of the incentive system to keep the rental housing stock up-to-date. In the current capital market situation the incentive seems too generous, however. There is a risk of overinvestment and in some locations unnecessary gentrification pressure has resulted. It should thus be considered to index the levy rate, i.e. to bind it to the rate of inflation. A markup of about 6 per cent upon the inflation rate should be sufficient.

A central problem of the German housing system is the severe market split between ongoing contracts and new contracts, especially in tight markets (see below, 4.2.6 and 4.2.7): In ongoing contracts the rental price laws are largely respected and provide for a significant rent-capping effect in tight markets, but the laws are literally meaningless for the newly concluded tenancies. This has resulted in huge rental price differences for comparable housing quality in tight housing markets.

There is also evidence of functional disturbances of the system. In fact, a growing number of urban housing markets in economic growth regions seem to be functionally impaired in the sense that they cannot find back into an equilibrium state by themselves. Thus the adaptational flexibility of the system should not be reduced further by closer rent ceilings. The current degree of market orientation of the LRR system should certainly not be reduced. The LRR should reflect market conditions and follow the movements of rents for new leases with not too much delay.

Currently, the German housing policy is again at a turning point. The worsening housing shortages in more and more cities force politicians to act. The answer of the new coalition is tighter regulation for the most part – against a background of an already highly regulated system. A noticeable increase in subsidies to compensate for the consequences of tightening the regulatory screw or to direct investment has, however, not taken place.

It is advisable to effectively limit the worsening market split effects. The legislator should put the teeth back into § 5 Wirtschaftsstrafgesetz (provision against undue rent increases, see below, 4.2.6) and at the same time provide for more flexibility of the rules determining the LRR by allowing market forces to play a bigger role. Concretely, the normative share of newly agreed rents should be specified in advance at 25 per cent at least[2] and the rents for new leases should be effectively capped at a level of 25 per cent above the LRR. Also, it could be introduced that only rents agreed upon or changed in the last two years should be included in the LRR calculation, thus increasing the market orientation of the LRR.

The effect would be that sitting tenants would have to pay a little more rent in tight market conditions, whereas tenants who sign a new treaty would be significantly relieved. According to a simulation calculation the maximum yearly percentage increase of the LRR under the rules proposed would be about 3.5 per cent.

The new coalition wants to limit the rents for new leases in cities with tight housing markets for a period of five years to a level of only 10 per cent above the respective LRRs (see Koalitionsvertrag 2013, p. 115). Currently, there is no effective limitation on the rents for new residential leases. The author also doubts that there will be one in the future.

A stronger restriction of rents in communities where a particularly large housing deficit is believed to prevail, would entail a substantial impairment of the signaling function of rental prices (SVR 2013, p. 463). Also, we should not forget, that local housing scarcities as such can only be cured by additional completions[3] (SVR 2013, p. 467) or a shrinking number of households and not by regulatory interference in rental price formation.

As our simulations have shown, an *effective* restriction of the rents for new leases to a level of only 10 per cent above the respective LRRs would have a significant impact on rental price formation: the factually uncapped newly

---

[2] In the Berlin Mietspiegel, the proportion of newly concluded rents is random, but representative: The 2012 Mietspiegel has a share of rents from newly concluded leases of 41 per cent.

[3] Not to forget conversions and the splitting of dwellings.

agreed rents are currently the only dynamic element in the adjustment process of LRRs to market conditions. They thus have a lead function for the formation of the LRR. Otherwise, the system is self-referential and inadaptive. The LRR thus requires a certain degree of market split and would largely lose its medium-term market orientation and in effect degenerate to a first generation type of administered rent if newly agreed rents were *effectively* capped to a level of only 10 per cent above the LRR. The regulation-induced functional failures, i.e. the disability of more and more local housing markets to find back into equilibrium, would be severely exacerbated. If effective, such a tight rent cap would also increase the pressure on tenants in the form of more expensive upgrades and conversions into condominiums. Also an increase in the share of stepped rent leases would have to be expected.

But how can the legislator make the rent caps for new leases effective? The purely civil law approach chosen is questionable. Probably, a large part of the tenants will accept excessive rent demands when concluding the lease, but without exercising their right to reduce the rent to the level permitted by the law afterwards. It is therefore suggested to rebalance the proposed rent caps on new leases. If their effectiveness could be secured, then they would not have to be so narrow to achieve the desired effect. If effectively reinforced, a rent cap of 25 per cent on new leases would be enough.

The critical point is to ensure the effectiveness of the price controls, however. That will not be possible without significant enforcement costs. It would be necessary to establish a new price authority. One could make the conclusion of leases subject to approval by the price authority, or at least give the tenant the possibility to have his lease checked with regard to the legal admissibility of the price agreed upon. Also, one should not a priori refrain from a criminal prosecution of infringements.

1.4   Incentives for new residential construction

The partial regulatory flexibilisation proposed here should be accompanied by spatially targeted incentives for new residential completions. The taxation of income from letting property and owner-occupied housing seems appropriate. A return to the declining balance depreciation is not recommended, because housing is not scarce everywhere. A misallocation of scarce resources would be the inevitable result if those depreciation allowances were to be reintroduced. In addition, the incidence problem should not be neglected. This is especially true for the proposal to focus the declining balance depreciation on the hot spots of housing needs. In tight markets improved depreciation allowances would lead to rising land prices because of the presumably lower elasticity of land supply. In addition, the depreciation instrument is anything but distribution neutral.

Therefore regionally targeted investment allowances or regionally targeted cheap KfW mortgage credit or additional subsidies for social housing should make a more effective use of public resources. But in order to induce new residential construction on a larger scale,

- the supply of residential land must be increased or the existing land be utilized more effectively (for example, by the mobilization of conversion land or high-density residential development which reduces the cost of land per square meter) and
- the construction costs should be limited effectively (for example, by process innovations, tax reductions or the dismantling of building regulations[4]).

It should be considered, to promote especially cost-effective urban housing developments with an intelligent investment allowance, which would decrease with rising construction and land costs per square meter.

From a long-term perspective more preventive action of housing policy is recommended in view of the slow speed of adjustment of the housing markets. Housing policy must provide for the necessary incentives and resources for new residential construction (land, building capacity) in a timely and regionally targeted manner.

---

[4] According to the empirical study of ARGE / / eV, the change of the legal requirements had the strongest impact on residential construction costs since 2000, in particular the value added tax increase in 2007, the constant increases in the real estate transfer tax, the Energy Saving Ordinance-tightening of 2002 and 2009 and the new requirements for barrier-free construction.

1.5   The role of social housing

The lack of affordable housing in places with many low-income inhabitants, low vacancy rates and high rent levels should be addressed with an intelligent mix of spatially targeted instruments. This includes social housing subsidies. Otherwise there is a risk that jobs especially in the low wage service sector cannot be occupied. The increasing shortage of affordable housing is thus likely to weaken the labor markets of the German growth centers (Pestel-Institut 2013, p. 3).

At first sight, the number of social dwellings (about 1.6 Million) seems low for a housing stock of more than 40 million units. This is partly compensated by the housing stock still belonging to the public sector. However, since the state is ultimately responsible for the really difficult cases and this task cannot be easily delegated to the private sector, further privatizations of dwellings, at least in places with many low-income inhabitants, should be more the exception than the rule.

States such as Bavaria, Schleswig-Holstein, Hamburg and North Rhine-Westphalia understand how to direct social housing funds to the locations where affordable housing is particularly scarce. However, it should be ensured that the social rents are at the bottom edge of the respective LRRs. A social compensation can be attained by an income-orientation of social housing programs. Also, the programs should be designed attractively and be open especially to private investors. In general, it seems appropriate in the current situation to increase funding for social housing and to provide for a needs-based distribution among the states and regions.

In order to limit the negative impact on spatial mobility and to enhance the effectiveness of the use of public resources devoted to social housing, an effective sanctioning of misallocations is recommended, provided that this has no adverse impact on the social composition of the tenants in a settlement. The short-term maturities of the younger social housing programs have already mitigated the misallocation problem to a certain extent, however. In addition, it is suggested to create an online exchange market for social dwellings enabling social tenants to exchange their current social dwelling against another one in a different town.

2 Definition of the PRS

The German private rental sector is comparatively large. It accounts for almost 80 per cent of the rental, and for more than 40 per cent of the total housing market. As in many other countries, individual private landlords dominate in the German PRS, especially in rural areas and suburbs. Corporate landlords account for 13 per cent of all rented dwellings and 17 per cent of the private rental housing stock (see below, 3.1 for further details).

The distinction between private and social renting[5] is relatively complicated in the German case. To start with, there are almost no not-for-profit suppliers. The public housing organizations (i.e. owned by territorial entities, usually cities or municipalities) have private legal forms (usually GmbH = Ltd.), are subject to general tax and rental laws and are usually expected to make profits and distribute part of them. Since they are also often expected to deliver a kind of social return it would not be adequate however to include the public housing stock into the definition of the private rental sector.

On the other hand, an important part of the social housing stock is owned by private suppliers who seek profit from their social housing stock, too. In the German case the author would prefer to define the PRS according to ownership. A dwelling would thus belong to the PRS if it is owned by a private person, a group of private persons or by a private company (listed and non-listed housing companies, insurance companies, open- and closed-end property funds, etc.) without a public shareholding and if the dwelling is not subject to social housing subsidies and regulation. Thus the PRS comprises all privately owned rental dwellings minus the privately owned social dwellings.[6] The problem is however that there are no exact numbers

---

[5] A common definition of social housing is: Government measures to subsidize housing for the support of households who cannot provide for suitable housing on the market, with the aim of supplying rental housing via the subsidization of investors or owner-occupied housing by subsidizing individuals under the framework of the respective federal or state law (Wohnraumförderungsgesetze).

[6] Large listed housing companies like LEG, Gagfah and Deutsche Annington have a considerable part of social dwellings in their housing stock.

available on the privately owned social housing stock. Thus the numbers used here can only reflect the ownership structures.

3   Structure of the housing market

3.1   Stock composition

The most striking characteristic of the German private rental sector from a comparative perspective is its size: almost 80 per cent of the rental, and more than 40 per cent of the total housing market.

Year	Owner-occu-pied	Individ-ual private rental	Private compa ny	Total private rental	public	Coop-eratives	other	Total dwell-ings
1993	13,02 (38,0%)	12,10 (35,3%)	2,19 (6,4%)	14,29 (41,7%)	3,60 (10,5%)	2,24 (6,5%)	1,10 (3,2%)	34,25 (100%)
2005	15,13 (39,1%)	13,79 (35,6%)	2,60 (6,7%)	16,39 (42,4%)	3,13 (8,1%)	2,29 (5,9%)	1,75 (4,5%)	38,69 (100%)
2011[7]	17,49 (42,3%)	13,90 (33,7%)	2,90 (7,0%)	16,80 (40,7%)	2,62 (6,3%)	2,11 (5,1%)	2,28[8] (5,5%)	41,30 (100%)

Table 3.1: Supply side structure of the German housing market over time: number of dwellings per group of landlords and per cent of total number of dwellings

As in many other countries, individual private landlords rather than property companies and financial institutions dominate in the German PRS. Private individuals account for 64 per cent of all rented dwellings and 83 per cent of privately rented dwellings. As elsewhere, they are a very heterogeneous group of actors in the housing market with diverse aims and backgrounds. However, they are predominantly self-employed or pensioners. The vast majority are amateur landlords with less than 15 dwellings who self-manage their portfolio. About half were purchased and just under half were inherited. They have a very long-term investment horizon and a marked preference for security of investment. In urban areas, professional landlords tend to dominate in the private rental market, but in

---

[7] Numbers from zensus 2011, see Statistisches Bundesamt 2013a.

[8] Dwellings owned by non-profit organizations plus holiday apartments and vacant dwellings.

17

rural areas and suburbs small-scale operators are often more common (BBSR 2012).

Corporate landlords account for 13 per cent of all rented dwellings and 17 per cent of the private rental housing stock. This includes private housing companies, insurance companies, pension funds and property funds. Since the late 1990s a number of large-scale financial investor property companies, many of which are owned by global private equity companies, have entered the PRS. They have built up large housing portfolios by taking over housing companies from public sector organizations and manufacturing firms.[9]

But how were these distinct supply side structures formed? On the eve of World War I a share of the PRS of 90 per cent of the total housing stock was typical in industrialized countries (Department of Environment 1977 and Howenstine 1981, p. 38). A long-term decline in the significance of private renting could be ascertained in most developed industrial countries since then. This development, however, was much less pronounced in Germany. In the first half of the 20th century still, the small private landlords were by far the largest landlord group in Germany. Even the boom of social housing construction in the postwar decades has not put the dominance of the private landlord in question.[10]

The other side of the coin of the large German rental sector is a low homeownership rate by international comparison (currently about 46 per cent[11]). Since the late eighties however, the rate of homeownership is moving upward. Not surprisingly, the average German homeownership rate is subject to significant regional differentiation.[12]

---

[9] Kofner, 2006, 2009, TRAWOS 2012.

[10] In 1961, the share of small private landlords was 42.7 per cent in the total housing stock and 64,5 per cent in the rental housing stock. There is evidence of an even larger market share in 1950 (Statistisches Bundesamt 2000, tables 6 and 70).

[11] Homeownership rates of comparable countries like Japan, the U.S., Belgium, France, Italy, Ireland and the U.K. range between 57 and 79 per cent.

[12] The share of tenants is particularly high in large parts of Eastern Germany, in northern North Rhine-Westphalia and in certain urban areas such as Berlin, with a tenant share of 87 percent. Quite different are the conditions in the Saarland, where the homeownership rate is 63 percent.

	1950	1961	1972	1982	1987	1993	1998	2002	2006	2010
Germany						38,8	40,9	42,6	41,6	45,7
West	39,1	33,8	35,8	40,4	39,3	41,7	43,1	44,6	44,6	48,8
East						26,4	31,2	34,2	30,6	34,4

Table 3.2: Homeownership rates[13] for Germany,
source: Statistisches Jahrbuch 2010 and BMVBS 2012.

The number of social dwellings is currently only 1.6 Million and still further shrinking. Thus, the sector is just a shadow of its former self. The total number of social dwellings once was above 4 Million dwellings. The declining importance of social housing is due to the reduction of federal subsidies and to the temporary character of the subsidies. However, an important part of the former social dwellings still belong to the public housing sector.

Year	Social housing stock Million dwellings	Percentage of total housing stock
1968	3.7	18,9
1987	4.0	15,3
2003	2.1	6,8
2013	1.6	3,9

Table 3.3: Long-term development of the social housing sector in Germany
Source: IWU 2005

The remaining social housing stock is owned by public and private landlords as well. Some social dwellings are also owned by not-for-profit actors. Private landlords either have developed their social housing stock themselves after having successfully applied for a social housing program or they have acquired former public interest housing organizations from the factory housing or public housing sector.

---

[13] Statistical concept „homeownership rate": Share of owner-occupied dwellings in all occupied dwellings in residential buildings.

3.2   Tenant profiles

The homeownership rates by age groups reflect the fact that German first time buyers / builders are relatively old as compared to other countries. Households under 30 have a home ownership rate of less than 10 per cent. Even in the age group of 30-40 year olds, the homeownership rate is only about 30 per cent.[14] Thus, the majority of younger and middle-aged households are tenants in Germany.

There is also a functional dependence between household size and homeownership rates. Whilst the homeownership rate of 1-person-households (the largest group of households) is 28 per cent, it is above 50 per cent in all other groups and rises with household size. Thus, the smaller the household, the higher the probability that it is a tenant household.

Also, not surprisingly, there is a clear correlation of homeownership and income. In the group with household income above 4,500 Euro the homeownership rate is 75 per cent. In the income class 3,200 - 4,500 Euro about two thirds of the households have a home of their own. In those income groups there is a potential for raising the homeownership rate since affordability we can presuppose as given in most cases.

On the other hand poorer households tend to be tenants. 71 per cent of the households with an income below 2,000 Euro are tenants.

3.3   Housing costs for tenants in the PRS

The average gross cold rent per m^2 and month was 6,37 Euro in 2010 (Statistisches Bundesamt 2013b). Ranked by state the rent level was highest in Hamburg (8,12 Euro) and lowest in Thuringia (5,47 Euro). The average rent burden was 22,8 per cent. Households receiving housing allowances ("Wohngeld") had a rent burden of 40 per cent before and 30 per cent after receipt of housing allowances.

According to data from Sozioökonomisches Panel (SOEP, see DIW 2013), the average housing cost burden (gross warm) in 2011 was 18 per cent for West German homeowners and 34 per cent for West German tenants. The

---

[14] Source: Statistisches Bundesamt, Zusatzerhebung zum Mikrozensus 2010. See Annex.

average housing cost burden (gross cold) in 2011 was 13 per cent for West German homeowners and 28 per cent for West German tenants.[15]

Housing costs (gross warm) per m² and month were 4,26 Euro for West German homeowners and 8,03 Euro for tenants (gross cold: 3,23 and 6,70 Euro, respectively). In absolute numbers the homeowners had gross warm housing costs of 494 Euro per month (gross cold: 373 Euro) and the tenants had gross warm housing costs of 581 Euro per month (gross cold: 485 Euro).

To the knowledge of the author, there are no data available that differentiate by landlord groups. However, the GdW member companies charged an average rent of 5,04 Euro per m² and month in 2012 plus 1,39 Euro for cold and 1,08 Euro for warm extra costs. We can conclude that in the PRS the average rent level will be slightly higher. To the knowledge of the author, no separate data are available about the housing costs of social housing tenants. We can assume however, that they will be significantly lower than in the PRS, especially for tenants with a long time of residence in the same dwelling.

It is noticeable, that the homeowners have absolutely lower housing costs than the tenants, even though they benefit from a quantitatively and qualitatively higher level of consumption. Their relative housing cost burden is even much lower than that of the tenants. These results can be explained by the higher income level of homeowners and a relatively low level of mortgage debt.

---

[15] The housing costs (gross cold) include for owners the cost components principal and interest on mortgage loans, cold operating costs (waste, water, street cleaning, etc.) and "Hausgeld" (allocation of costs for property management, etc.) [only since 1991], for tenants the cost components net rent and cold operating costs. The housing costs (gross warm) include for owners and tenants, housing costs (gross cold) plus the cost of heating and hot water (surveyed in the SOEP only from 1986).

3.4 Turnover rates

The availability of current data is rather limited in this field. According to the Berlin Senate's administration the fluctuation rate in Berlin is currently just below 10 per cent and falling.

The housing industry association GdW (representing public, cooperative and most of the large listed landlords) determined for 2012 an average fluctuation rate of 9.2 per cent (2005: 10.3). In the West, the turnover rate was 8.6 per cent (2005: 9.7), in the new Länder, however, it stood at 10.0 per cent (2005: 11.2). In Bavaria, the rate was only at 6.5 per cent in 2012 (GdW 2013, p. 153).[16] There are indications that even in cities with extremely low vacancy rates the turnover rates are still at a bearable level. A case in point is Hamburg with according to GdW data a vacancy rate of 0.8 per cent and a turnover rate of 7.8 per cent. This tight housing market is probably still not completely closed thus – at least for the better-off immigrants.

The average residence time in the social housing stock and in owner-occupied housing is likely to be significantly higher than 7.5 years.

The data also suggest that the fluctuation is lower than the average in housing cooperatives and higher among the tenants of small private landlords.

There is thus some evidence that private renting is the most flexible tenure. This is no surprise since the other tenures are marked by rent advantages and / or relatively high transaction costs.

---

[16] According to data from the meter reading company techem the overall fluctuation rate was 13.3 per cent in 2012 (only state capitals included). The fluctuation rates vary considerably between the state capitals. In my estimation, these data are not representative. I suspect that the turnover rate in the overall housing stock is significantly lower. On the other hand the GdW data may understate the fluctuation given the considerable share of social dwellings in their stock.

4 Policies and reforms that impact the PRS

4.1 Driving forces and winners / losers of housing reform

We can identify certain policy milestones which have fundamentally reshaped the housing market and also had important implications for the PRS (see Kofner 2003):

- 1950: With "Erstes Wohnungsbaugesetz" the privately financed newly constructed dwellings were excluded from rent control and special dismissal protection. A split market was established in order to provide incentives for new private residential development.

- 1960: With the "Abbaugesetz" all dwellings still under special legal protection were step by step released from rent control and dismissal protection. This law was the final fulfillment of the vision of a liberalized rental housing market always pursued by the governments since 1949.

- 1970/1971: A major turning point in German postwar housing policy. After a few years with almost unrestricted freedom of contract, general dismissal protection (see below, 4.3) and the local reference rent system (see below, 4.2.1) were introduced. Market intervention became permanent independent of the scarcity situation at the housing market. This has helped to foster demand among households for renting as a tenure since it was re-established as a reliable and long-term tenure.

- 1990: Public interest housing ("Wohnungsgemeinnützigkeit") was abolished. The companies belonging to that sector lost their tax advantages and gained in terms of entrepreneurial freedom. Since 1990 the companies could more easily than before sell apartments, increase rents, distribute profits to their owners or be sold themselves. The abolition of the public interest housing status was not least motivated by the expectation of higher tax revenues.

- 1990: German reunification: release of the central government from its central position in housing provision, decentralization and privatization of investment and financing decisions, market-oriented rent formation, heavy subsidies for new residential construction and stock modernization.

- January 1996: Conversion of home ownership subsidization from a tax to a grant system ("Eigenheimzulage"). The objectives were based on social and family policy considerations in particular. The system seemed to be heading for a new balance of tenures.

- January 2006: Abolition of the declining balance depreciation scheme for new residential developments and of the homeownership grant (Eigenheimzulage). Since then the German government tried to run the housing system with negligible subsidies by international comparison. The significant cuts in housing subsidies were a government initiative not primarily motivated by housing market-related reasoning. The corresponding changes were enforced against heavy resistance of the affected lobby groups (Woebken-Ekert 2005). The abolition of the homeownership grant was basically justified with the need to improve the budget situation of the public sector (draft bill, Bundestagsdrucksache 16/108, 29.11.2005).

The following table presents an overview of the main driving forces and the winners and losers of the milestone reform laws which have fundamentally shaped the German housing system.

Reform law	Main driving force	Winners	Losers
1950: Erstes Wohnungsbaugesetz	Background: Extreme housing shortage	Residential developers	Tenants of newly constructed and privately financed dwellings
1960: Abbaugesetz	Political vision / Ideology Background: Housing market relaxation	Landlords	Tenants
1970/1971: Fundamental reform of tenancy laws	Political vision / Ideology Social policy considerations: cap on rising rents	Tenants	Landlords
1990: Abolition of public interest housing	Increase of tax revenue Ideology of deregulation	Pubic interest landlords	Tenants
1990: German reunification	Extreme housing shortage: in terms of quantity and quality Social policy considerations: limit on rent adaptation	Residential developers Existing tenants	Tenants of newly constructed and privately financed dwellings
1996: Introduction of Eigenheimzulage	Social and family policy considerations: improve access to homeownership Background: Housing shortage	New homeowners with low or medium income	New homeowners with high income
2006: Abolition of the most important housing subsidies	Increase of tax revenue Background: Housing market relaxation		New homeowners Tenants Residential developers

Table 4.1: Winners and losers of the milestone reform laws

The housing market situation was of overwhelming importance in 1950 and 1990. As a policy background it was important in 1960, 1996 and 2006. The mix of measures taken would have been different or the measures would have been adopted at another time without the specific housing market situation prevailing in those three decisive years. For example: If a severe housing shortage had prevailed in 2006 the government would probably not have reduced the two most important subsidies for new residential development to zero at the same time.

Political ideology played a role in 1960, 1970/1971 and 1990. The decisions taken in these years reflected fundamentally different views of the role of the state in the housing market and in the wider economy. It is important to note that the interventionist school of thought has prevailed in this clash of ideologies.

Social policy considerations have shaped decisions in 1970/1971, 1990 and 1996. In 1970/1971 and 1990 it was considered important to have a firm grip on the future path of rent development. In 1996 housing reform was aiming at a distribution of homeownership less dependent on income strata.

The political aim of improving the tax revenue situation was important in 1990 (abolition of public interest housing) and 2006. The decision to abolish the two most important housing subsidies at the same time was a fundamental change of political priorities.

4.2   How rents are set

The rent regulation relating to the publicly owned housing stock depends on the status of the dwellings. For social dwellings the relevant laws and program rules apply and for the rest of the stock general rental laws apply. There is no federal or state regulation focusing on specific types of providers.

The basis of the German system of rent price formation is the local reference rent (abbreviated "LRR" in the following) – an average of the prices competing landlords demand for dwellings of comparable quality. The quality comparison is however limited to certain normative criteria, i.e. type of dwelling, location, size, constructual condition and equipment of the apartment. The LRR acts as an upper limit for the permissible rent in ongoing contracts.

The LRR is an artificial concept not to be confused with a market rent. The rules for its calculation have the effect that the LRR reflects the younger history of the local housing market and not the current market situation. But as such it is a market-oriented rent system and very different from the

Dutch system of rent-setting, which was not oriented towards any market value.

There are other factors determining rent levels apart from the LRR. The costs for the modernization of a dwelling have direct consequences for the maximum permissible rent, but those rent increases are unconnected with the LRR system.

What is more, the LRR is the most common, but not the only admissible contractual framework for the determination of future rent increases. There are two more: the index-linked rent and the stepped rent.

4.2.1 Local reference rent and Mietspiegel

The calculation of the LRR includes rents from new leases as well as rent increases in existing contracts, but excludes rents from ongoing rental contracts which were not raised. The LRR behaves relatively independently of the development of rents from new leases in the short and medium term. The reasons for the delay in adapting are in particular:

- Inclusion of rents *from ongoing contracts* when changed (§ 558 para 2 sentence 1 BGB),
- Inclusion of rents agreed upon or changed *in the last four years* (ibid.),
- Compliance with the *rent caps* (§ 558 para 3 BGB),
- Often delayed adjustment of the rental index ("Mietspiegel") to market developments.

Given these built-in delay factors, the landlord can profit from windfall gains in ongoing contracts only in a medium- or long-term perspective. Also, the effect of the LRR on price formation depends not least upon the local practice of determining the LRR.

In this regard, the "Mietspiegel" are of great importance. The LRR is a legal concept which refers to the empirical rent structure of the (local) housing market. A Mietspiegel on the other hand is an instrument (there are more: databases, expert assessment, set of reference dwellings) for surveying and exhibiting the LRR structure in a community. The Mietspiegel is often empirically based and in most cases it has a table structure according to criteria like location, equipment and size of the dwelling.[17] It helps landlords and tenants to find the adequate reference rent for a particular dwelling. The main function of the Mietspiegel is the improvement of transparency and legal certainty for the rent increase process. The Mietspiegel do not necessarily reflect the LRR correctly, however. This is subject to court ruling.

Since there are almost no legally binding methodological rules each city uses its own structure and methodology which makes the whole system rather intransparent. Furthermore, since it is not compulsory for German cities to have a Mietspiegel, many small and medium size cities and some larger cities have no Mietspiegel at all.

The German Civil Code also knows "qualified" Mietspiegel, which have the legal presumption on their side to reflect the LRR correctly. They have to be in accordance with accepted scientific principles (i.e. empirically-representative), to be recognized by the community or the interest groups (§ 558d BGB, para 1) and to be adjusted to market development at least every two years. Hence qualified Mietspiegel are an ideal source of evidence in a rent increase court process. The dissemination of qualified Mietspiegel is still low, however.[18]

Since the mid-70s, Mietspiegel have become increasingly prevalent in Germany. Currently, 701 municipalities refer to the data from approximately 350 Mietspiegel, 86 thereof are qualified. Their dissemination depends on the size of the municipality. Whilst only 0.7 per cent of the communities with less than 20,000 inhabitants maintain a Mietspiegel, about 60 per cent of the communities with a number of inhabitants between 50,000 and 100,000 people and almost 90 per cent of the communities with more than 100,000 inhabitants do so. The size class between 20,000 and 50,000 inhabitants exhibits a mixed picture: 26 per cent have a Mietspiegel

---

[17] A Mietspiegel has to be structured according to the housing quality characteristics enumerated in § 558 BGB. It has to be created or recognized either by the municipality or by representatives of interest of landlords and tenants in common (§ 558c para 1 BGB).

[18] Even among municipalities with more than 100,000 inhabitants less than a third have one. Among smaller communities qualified Mietspiegel are an exception. This is a reflection of the considerable costs to maintain a qualified Mietspiegel.

of their own and another 15 per cent refer to Mietspiegel from other communities. Mietspiegel thus rarely occur in small towns.[19]

In places where there is no Mietspiegel rents are raised referring to a set of reference dwellings or expert assessments. Presumably the reference dwellings are the most common method. It must be the lowest rent of a minimum of three dwellings and the landlord may take the reference dwellings from his own rental housing stock. It should be noted that in case of a lawsuit the judge will not presume that the reference dwellings correctly represent the LRR. In general, markets without a Mietspiegel are not transparent, neither for the landlords, nor for the tenants. It is not easy to explain why the LRR regulation is applied without appropriate tools for the determination of the reference rent.

4.2.2 Rent caps

The scope of permissible rent increases in ongoing contracts is not only limited by the LRR, but also by an additional rent cap (§ 558 para 3 BGB) which limits the scope for rent increases over three years to a maximum of 20 per cent. The tenant can reduce the rent to the permissible amount in case of exceedance. The state governments can denominate municipalities with severe housing shortages where the maximum rate is only 15 per cent.[20]

The rent cap limit even applies if a comparison with the relevant LRR would permit a higher rent increase. Rent increases within the three-year limit that were legitimately made due to modernization activities or increased operating costs remain unconsidered whatsoever.

---

[19] BBSR-Fachbeitrag Mietspiegel,
http://www.bbsr.bund.de/BBSR/DE/WohnenImmobilien/Immobilienmarktbeobachtung/ProjekteFachbeitraege/Mietspiegel/Mietspiegel.html

[20] The lower rent cap has only been introduced recently, so that definitive conclusions about their distribution are not possible. It seems that the number of cities and neighborhoods where a lower rent cap applies still further increases. In Berlin and Hamburg the lower rent cap applies throughout the whole city. In North Rhine-Westphalia, an empirical report was commissioned to identify the areas where an adequate supply of the population with rental housing on reasonable terms is particularly endangered.

The rent cap seems not compatible with the idea of market-based rent determination. However, the development of the LRRs usually does not allow for rent increases of such magnitude.

The rent caps will primarily be a problem for the housing industry, when rent controls expire (e.g. a dwelling losing its status of a social dwelling). In such cases the rent cap prevents a rapid catch-up of the formerly controlled rents. The rent caps are usually justified by the fact that the tenant should not be surprised by rent jumps to which they could not adjust economically.

4.2.3 Apportionment of modernization costs

Landlords can impose incurred modernization costs on their tenants in yearly portions. The modernization apportionment is a central instrument for keeping the housing stock in good condition with respect to contemporary technical standards. This is especially true for the climate- and the age-appropriate adaptation of the housing stock. However, the modernization allocation fulfills the function of an accelerator of gentrification processes in some places. In low-demand regions on the other hand, the landlord may not be able to collect full compensation for the modernization costs incurred. The modernization apportionment is not limited to measures enhancing the functional value or the general living conditions, but also includes measures to save energy, heating costs and water.

The levying of a surcharge after a modernization legally requires the tenant's obligation to tolerate the corresponding measures of the landlord. The hardship for the tenant and the legitimate interests of the landlord and the other tenants have to be weighed thoroughly.[21]

By unilateral declaration the landlord may add 11 per cent of the modernization costs (excluding financing and maintenance costs) to the annual rent.[22] This option is an alternative to a rent increase based on the

---

[21] The law has specified the term hardship: The "works carried out", the "structural effects", "previous investments of the tenant" and the "expected increase of the rent" (except for production of general standard) are qualified as possible hardship reasons.

[22] According to prevailing legal opinion if the rent is raised on the basis of § 559 BGB the rent caps and the 20 per cent limit of § 5 WiStG need not be taken into account.

LRR. In most cases the modernization apportionment enables higher rent increases than would have been possible under the reference rent system.

The tenant is obliged to pay the modernization apportionment until the next rent increase based on the LRR. In the event of a change of the tenant the new tenant does not have to pay the levy. Regardless of the previous rent level, the rent must then be renegotiated under the statutory provisions.

The rigidity of the 11 per cent allocation rate is open to criticism. Depending on the development of capital market interest rates modernizations are either postponed or accelerated at the cost of the tenants. In the current capital market situation residential modernization is a very profitable business, if the landlord can collect the full 11 per cent modernization apportionment.

The modernization apportionment is only one element of the incentive system for the modernization of residential buildings. The tax treatment of such investments was always generous (see below, chapter 4.4). Also, since 2000 low-interest loans from the KfW bank for measures raising the energy efficiency of residential buildings are available and since 2009 also KfW loans for the age-appropriate conversion of existing housing stock.

4.2.4   Stepped rent

The stepped rent is a form of rent, where the extent and the timing of future rent increases is determined in advance. The future rent steps have to be disclosed in the lease agreement in absolute terms (§ 557a para 1 BGB). This can be done for example in the following form: "The net rent is increased annually, from 1 January 2013 to 820 €, from 1 January 2014 to 840 €, from 1 January 2015 to 860 €, etc."

The increased rent is due at the given time, without further payment request by the landlord. Further rent increases – including modernization-linked increases - are excluded during the term of the stepped lease. The LRR is only taken into account if an excessively high price is charged (practically irrelevant, see below, 4.2.6). The rent caps (maximum rent increase of 20 per cent in 3 years) are not applicable.

Step rent agreements can be combined with an exclusion of the tenant's right to terminate the lease agreement with due notice. The tenant's right to terminate can be ruled out for up to four years. This regulation serves the landlord's certainty in calculation. But it also affects the tenants by limiting their mobility to a considerable extent. It therefore needs to be put under scrutiny.

As compared to the LRR, the landlord can generate higher rental income in the medium run by concluding a stepped rent.

As compared with the index-linked rent the stepped rent is the more familiar and more widely used alternative (Kletečka / Oberhammer / Wall 2011, p. 55). Nevertheless, the proportion of all leases is likely to be still in the single digit figures. The LRR is still the standard model for rent increases in existing contracts.

The stepped rent has yet a kind of valve function for the system. If the legal rent ceilings with regard to the LRR were further exacerbated, the market share of stepped rent contracts is likely to rise further.

4.2.5 Index-linked rent

In the case of an indexation of the rent a link between the contractual rent and the price index for all households published by the Federal Statistical Office in Wiesbaden is established. The future rent is therefore not fixed, but depends on the development of the consumer price index. Here, however, the provisions of § 557b BGB and § 2 Price Clause Law ("Preisklauselgesetz") are relevant: In case of a decline in the index the contract rent has to be reduced (symmetry) and no disproportionate percentage change in the contractual rent as compared to the percentage change of the index is allowed (proportionality).

In contrast to the stepped rent the assertion of a rent increase requires a written statement from the landlord (§ 557b para 3 BGB). A rent increase under § 559 (modernization apportionment) may only be required if the landlord had to invest under circumstances for which he was not responsible. A rent increase with reference to the LRR is excluded.

According to market participants, the index-linked rent is rarely used in practice. The proportion of index leases in all residential tenancy agreements is likely to be in the low single digits.

4.2.6 Enforcement of the rent controls

The legislator has made provision against the circumvention of the price controls. It is no alternative to adjust the rent via a chain of short-term rental agreements. According to § 575 BGB, a "tenancy for a fixed period" can only be concluded into if the landlord has a legitimate interest in it (e.g. future personal need of the dwelling or foreseeable substantial changes of the construction) and if he had informed the tenant already when the agreement was concluded. The possibility to adjust the rent with a notice of termination pending a change of the contract (i.e. the price per square meter) is also legally excluded (§ 573 paragraph 1 sentence 2 and Section 2 No. 3 BGB).

There are regulatory provisions against major exceedances of the LRR. A rent charge is regarded as inappropriate ("Mietpreisüberhöhung", § 5 Wirtschaftsstrafgesetz WiStG) if the landlord "exploits" a market situation where the availability of comparable dwellings is limited by demanding or taking a rent which exceeds the LRR by more than 20 per cent.

The Criminal Code contains another rule against the charging of excessively high prices: Rack-renting ("Mietwucher") refers to a conspicuous disparity between performance and reward. Such a disparity is assumed as a rule, if the rent demanded exceeds the customary rent (i.e. the LRR) by more than 50 per cent. The Mietwucher (usury) paragraph 291 of the German Criminal Code requires other constituent elements: exploitation of predicament, inexperience, lack of judgement or significant weakness of will on the part of the lessee.

Mietpreisüberhöhung according to § 5 WiStG has in practice only a very small significance. In Hamburg (a very large city with a very tight housing market for years) there were no proceedings of Mietpreisüberhöhung pending in early March 2012.[23] According to the Berlin Senate's

---

[23] Answer of the Senate of Hamburg to a corresponding small request (Drucksache 20/3358

administration the same was true for Berlin in late November 2013. In 2011, only two cases of Mietwucher were pending in Hamburg and no cases were recorded in Berlin in November 2013.

It is thus probable that in other big cities the number of corresponding administrative proceedings is also very low. Also, according to the observations of the German Tenants' Association (DMB) and the housing industry association GdW, § 5 WiStG is practically ineffective. This development has been promoted decisively by the jurisdiction.[24]

Thus there is no effective protection against excessive rent demands for newly established tenancies even if they go very far beyond the LRR. The LRR has no practical value for new tenancies, as the rules are not enforced. This is surprising given the housing shortages in many cities. The result is a market split in tight markets with huge differences between the existing rents and the newly agreed rents for comparable housing quality.

But then the housing markets would have to be cleared. Since the markets of cities like Munich, Hamburg and Frankfurt am Main with vacancy rates below 1 per cent are all but cleared, the only possible conclusion is that *the landlords use their pricing power only to a limited extent.*

4.2.7 Assessment of the impact of the rent controls

The long-term impact of the LRR system on local rent levels depends on the local housing market situation. In cities such as Zwickau, where the housing market is relaxed, quoted rents and LRRs are close together, whereas in tight housing markets huge differences can occur. The table below exhibits the percentage deviations between average local reference and quoted rents for various German cities.

---

v. 02.03.2012).

[24] To this situation, particularly the Bundesgerichtshof (BGH, highest civil court) has contributed with two decisions of 2004 and 2005 (BGH VIII ZR 190_03 and BGH VIII ZR 44_04). It is here above all the question, what does "exploitation of an insufficient supply of housing" exactly means. According to the BGH, the low supply must be valid in the quality segment in question across the entire city and not just in the neighbourhood or district where the apartment is located. And besides, according to BGH the behaviour and the personal situation of the tenant are also important in this respect. In effect, the BGH has rendered § 5 WiStG ineffective.

City	Quoted rent for new tenancies €/m²	LRR €/m²	Percentage deviation
München	12.64	9.48	33.3
Frankfurt am Main	10.93	6.41	70.5
Hamburg	9.89	6.36	55.5
Heidelberg	9.68	6.56	47.6
Stuttgart	9.39	7.40	26.9
Düsseldorf	9.22	5.75 – 7.45[25]	39.7
Köln	9.17	7.93[26]	15.6
Münster	8.64	6.56[27]	31.7
Bonn	8.60	6.75	27.4
Zwickau	4.73	4.39	7.7
Gera	4.73	4.50	5.1
Bremerhaven	4.72	4.35	8.5

Table 4.2: Rents for new tenancies and local reference rents in selected German cities

Sources: F+B Mietspiegelindex, ImmobilienScout 24 and diverse Mietspiegel[28]

There is thus evidence for a noticeable effect of the rent controls in tight housing markets. In a market like Frankfurt am Main we observe the usual accompanying factors of a split market, i.e. large rent differences between market segments according to the degree of regulatory interference and low fluctuation rates among sitting tenants. The LRR will tend to rise in such a market and it may rise faster than the cost of living, but not enough to clear the market (the vacancy rate being 1.0 per cent). In fact, a full market

---

[25] Mietspiegel 2011.

[26] Average local reference rent according to F&B Mietspiegelindex 2012.

[27] Data retrieval Mietspiegel Münster: Adresses with medium locational quality, ready for occupancy 1975-1984. Size of dwelling: 65 m², no special characteristics, no modernizations after 31. December 1995.

[28] Data retrievals from Mietspiegel were based on a dwelling with 65 m², medium locational quality, construction year 1975, no special characteristics and thus no additions or deductions.

clearance would require far higher rents for new lettings, ceteris paribus. To be sure, second generation rent control systems allow for market clearance in principle, if the rents for new leases are unregulated as is currently the case in Germany. The German LRR system along with the reluctance of landlords in exploiting severe housing scarcities thus seem to delay considerably the process of market clearance in tight housing markets as long as the fundamental demand factors do not change.

Apart from that the market split presents a significant obstacle to spatial mobility especially in tight housing markets (often identical with the centers of economic growth). In such markets sitting tenants would give up their price advantage when moving. If a tenant of a privately financed dwelling say in Düsseldorf, who pays 50 per cent less than for a comparable new lease (say 6 € instead of 9 € per m^2 and month) wants to move to Frankfurt, then he will have a problem to find an apartment there, and even if he succeeds, he will most probably have to pay a much higher price per square meter for the new dwelling (maybe 11 €). Housing allowances if at all (subject to income and rent ceilings) will only cover part of his additional rent payments. This kind of regulation is prone to create a situation where, despite a low rate of home ownership, incentives to move are significantly impaired.

The factual price freedom for new leases on the other hand, taken by itself, promotes investment in new residential developments. A correction at this point thus would require improved incentives elsewhere, if it is to have a neutral impact on residential completions.

It is generally not recommendable to keep the rents in ongoing contracts substantially below the current rents for newly concluded tenancies. The deeper the regulatory market split, the higher the risk of pronounced and persistent demand overhangs with their undesirable side effects (random allocation, black markets). The sitting tenants thus should not be largely excluded from the housing market adjustment processes. If they are, they tend to consume too much housing space (an unnecessary waste of resources) and the households seeking a dwelling will carry too much of the adjustment burden in terms of transaction costs and higher rent prices for the same housing quality. This is simply unfair.

Another structural problem of the German LRR system is that the fluctuation rate has a considerable influence on the path of the LRR. The growth rate of the LRR slows down considerably in times of a local housing scarcity and thus the necessary adjustment of the market is postponed.

The LRR system is however a possible response to certain forms of market failure in housing markets. The relationship-specific investments of tenants (SVR 2013, p. 467) are worthy of protection since they provide scope for monopolistic pricing and that is an argument against adapting rents via notice of termination pending a change of the contract. Also, the low price elasticities of supply and demand which tend to amplify price swings may be regarded as a justification for a certain capping of the rents for new lettings.

The solution must be such that rents for both, existing and the newly signed leases are limited, but in terms of a fair burden sharing between insiders and outsiders and without putting the medium-term market orientation of the system and its ability to clear the market into question. It is however doubtful whether the solution proposed in the coalition agreement satisfies the second requirement: The new coalition wants to limit rents for new leases to a maximum of only 10 per cent above the LRR (currently 20 per cent, but ineffective) in cities with tight housing markets (to be chosen by the state governments) for a period of five years (presumably with a renewal option). Newly constructed dwellings shall be exempted however from the new rent ceiling. Also, the individual rent level already achieved, shall be "protected" (Koalitionsvertrag 2013, p. 115). Thus, existing rents would not have to be reduced and new rents could be concluded at least at the price level of the previous contract.

4.3   Dismissal protection

The "normal" (i.e. by far most widely used and legally preferred) type of residential lease agreement is a tenancy for an indefinite period of time. Such type of agreement can be terminated any time with due notice (but: the landlord is only permitted to do so in case of a legitimate interest on his side, see below). In a fixed-term lease on the other hand a termination during the term period is generally excluded. The conclusion of a fixed-term lease is however subject to strict legal requirements and only admissible in cases of exception (see above, 4.2.6).

Tenant and landlord can effectively agree upon a termination exclusion for a maximum period of four years.

4.3.1   Termination without notice

A termination without notice is only permitted in case of serious breaches of contract ("good cause"), resulting in "unreasonableness" of the continuation of the lease (§ 543 para 1 BGB). The German Civil Code contains an exhaustive enumeration of reasons for the immediate termination of a rental agreement. As reasons for a termination without notice by the tenant the law lists: Not granting the use and health hazards. The following reasons for a termination without notice by the landlord are recognized:

- Use contrary to the agreement (§ 543 para 2 No. 2 BGB). Examples: violation of the due diligence or unauthorized sub-letting.
- Neglect of duty of care. Examples: exposure to water damage or fire hazard or misuse.
- Unreasonable tenancy (§ 569 para 2 BGB). Example: repeated serious violations of house rules.
- Late payments (§ 543 para 2, No. 3 and § 569 paragraph 3 BGB).
- Termination for good reason: § 543 para 1 BGB

4.3.2   Dismissal with due notice

An ordinary termination of contract (§ 573) is also possible against contract loyal tenants. The landlord does not have a free right to terminate however. Termination is only permitted in cases of a "legitimate interest" (§ 573 para

1 sentence 1). If the landlord terminates the contract without having a legitimate interest in it, the termination is ineffective.

The dismissal protection is thus not limited to cases of hardship, it is general. It is also asymmetrical, because tenants are still allowed to ordinarily terminate the lease without having to indicate a proper reason. As an important secondary function this type of dismissal protection ensures the effectiveness of the rent controls.

A set of specific reasons is recognized as legitimate interest of the landlord by the law:

- Willful or negligent substantial breach of duty by the tenant: Cases in point are late payment, non-conforming use, unreasonable tenancy.
- Hindrance to economic exploitation (§ 573 paragraph 2, No. 3 BGB): almost insignificant in practice except for demolitions.
- Personal need of the landlord (§ 573 paragraph 2 No. 2): see below
- Conversion of adjoining rooms to living space
- Termination for good reason

The most common reason for proper termination of the contract is personal need. Personal need is when the landlord needs the dwelling for himself or for a person belonging to his household or for a family member for residential purposes. In case of dispute, the landlord must state and prove his personal needs.

The statutory provision of § 577a BGB stipulates that the termination of a lease agreement because of personal need is only possible after the expiry of 3 (or up to 10) years after the purchase of the apartment, if the property had been split into condominiums after the hand-over of the apartment to the tenant.

4.3.3   Contradiction of the tenant (§§ 574-574b)

Up to this point it can surely be concluded that tenancy protection is very strong in Germany. And on top of it, even if the landlord's cancellation is effective (legitimate), the tenant must not move out, if he is subject to hardship. The tenant can disagree in this case at least two months before the termination of the tenancy, the notice and demand the continuation of the lease. This "social clause" of § 574 BGB cannot be waived in the lease agreement (§ 574 para 4 BGB).

The termination must be an undue hardship for the tenant, even if the legitimate interests of the landlord are considered. In addition to the tenant and his family, other household members are protected, too, if they run a joint household with the tenant (spouse, foster children).

The following examples for individual hardship have been developed by case law: pregnancy, severe illness, low income, long residence time of elderly people, disability, infirmity, upcoming exams, difficulties in school and kindergarten changes, two moves within a short time, tenant investment (contractual or approved), non-availability of alternative accommodation on reasonable terms (§ 574 para 2).

If a hardship reason is valid the tenant is entitled to continuation of the tenancy for as long as is reasonable "taking into account all the circumstances" (§ 574a para 1 sentence 1). This may in certain cases (e.g. high age of the tenant and long residence time) mean that the tenancy will continue indefinitely. If the parties cannot agree, the court determines the conditions of the continuation of the lease.

4.3.4   Eviction procedures

In the German legal system, the landlord is not allowed to put a tenant just before the door. Even if a lease no longer exists because it has expired, or has been revoked or terminated, the landlord cannot forcibly remove simply the tenant. Also, the landlord may not change the locks of the dwelling.

If the tenant does not hand over the dwelling in due time, the evacuation of the apartment must be enforced. To do so a court order is required. In the legal proceedings, the court will convict the tenant to vacate the apartment because of the termination of the lease. Only with this court ruling, the evacuation of the apartment can be enforced.

The eviction is carried out by the bailiff. The considerable costs of an eviction have to be initially advanced by the creditor. They can be recovered later, however, as well as the cost of the eviction action from the debtor. Unfortunately, it ultimately turns out in many cases that the debtor is insolvent.

4.3.5 Assessment of the impact of dismissal protection

The tenancy protection rules are at the core of the construction of renting as a tenure. They are the basis for the well-justified expectation of every tenant that renting provides long-term security of tenure. Without asymmetrical dismissal protection renting would not be the first choice for households aiming for a long-term engagement. As in countries with weak tenant protection the rental sector would be the domain of the ones with short-term housing needs and the ones who cannot afford a home of their own. One can even say that dismissal protection *creates* an important part of the demand for renting as a tenure.

Thus the strong tenancy protection rules fundamentally affect the housing market. Once a rental agreement is concluded the landlord is in a structurally weak position. He could not even raise the rent, if he could not legally claim for rent increases up to the LRR level. The LRR system is in fact a consequence of the legislator's fundamental decision to provide general dismissal protection (or vice versa). The dismissal protection taken by itself is not a considerable disincentive to invest in the rental market, although private landlords may not be content with the related disposal restrictions.

Apart from that, dismissal protection has a negative effect on the turnover and the willingness to move. It provides an incentive for pecuniary and non-pecuniary investment of tenants in their dwellings and their social neighborhood. These contract-specific investments have a negative effect on mobility. In the perception of tenants as well as from a legal perspective the right to use the dwelling was transformed into something similar to a property-type right.[29] That goes very far – on the other hand: without

---

[29] The Federal Constitutional Court in its judgment of 26. May 1993 has contributed crucially to the positioning of a tenancy as a kind of ownership right (BVerfG, 26.05.1993 - 1BvR 208/93). The Federal Constitutional Court has referred to the right of possession of the tenant relating to the dwelling as a property right protected by Article 14 paragraph 1 of the German Grundgesetz (federal constitution).

intensive dismissal protection many households who are tenants today, would live in owner-occupied housing. That is, they would invest even more and their mobility would be even lower.

In Germany, there are currently no policy initiatives or discussions on deregulating the dismissal protection laws. These rules seem to be so deeply ingrained that it would be tantamount to political suicide to touch them.

4.4   Taxation of rental income

Important subsidies address to homeowners and landlords or tenants as well, e.g. tax incentives for monuments (for homeowners and landlords) or housing allowances (for homeowners and tenants). At first sight, there seem to be no subsidies specifically tailored to rental housing. As a matter of fact federal housing subsidies have been declining rapidly in recent years. The help is currently focused on specific issues like energetic modernization, senior-friendly reconstruction, preservation of buildings and urban redevelopment, but does not include general tax subsidies any more. The main features of the German tax system for private landlords are:

- Capital gains taxation privilege
- Mortgage interest relief
- Negative gearing
- Depreciation allowances (linear)
- Immediate deduction of repair expenses from rent income

Residential letting is taxed as an investment. Landlords pay tax on their rental income, but capital gains from the sale of residential buildings held privately for more than ten years are tax-free unless the seller is a "commercial real estate dealer" (i.e. a regular trader) or a corporation. Capital gains on real business assets may be transferred to "replacing assets" (i.e. newly built or acquired property). The treatment of capital gains from owner-occupied housing is even more generous, however. As compared with the tax treatment of capital gains on financial investments (25 per cent withholding tax, regardless of the holding period) rental housing is privileged nevertheless. In the current environment of rising house prices that may be an important investment motive for some buyers an builders.

Landlords are eligible for mortgage interest tax relief and may offset losses from rental property against their other sources of taxable income ("negative gearing").

Public housing companies use private legal forms and are thus subject to the same tax rules as their private competitors. Housing cooperatives do not pay income-related taxes, if more than 90 percent of their income stems from residential letting.

Income from social housing stock is taxed just as income from any other type of rental housing. There is no difference, neither in determining the tax base, nor with the tax rates.

Before the decreasing balance method of depreciation for new residential development was abandoned with effect from 1. January 2006, rental buildings were generally regarded as good tax-saving vehicles especially by self-employed people like master craftsmen and other higher earners. Since then income tax depreciation is linear with 2 or 2.5 per cent for older buildings, respectively. This should be consistent with economic depreciation by and large.

The tax system provides incentives to invest in the existing housing stock. Buildings under monumental protection and buildings located in statutory redevelopment or preservation areas benefit from a higher depreciation scheme.[30] The most important general tax subsidy for German landlords is the possibility to deduct repair expenses immediately from rent income under certain conditions.[31]

---

[30] As stipulated in § 7h resp. 7i of the German income tax law, i.e. 9 per cent per year in the first eight years after purchase

[31] For the question of whether maintenance expenses are immediately deductible or not, the BMF (Federal Ministry of Finance) letter dated 18.07.2003 is relevant (IV C 3 – S 2211 – 94/03). Even if in two of four fields (heating installation, plumbing, electrical installation, windows) an increased standard is achieved by the set of measures, the entire cost would still be deductible immediately.

4.5 Homeownership subsidies

Mortgage interest is not deductible in the German owner-occupied sector because for tax purposes the home is regarded as a consumption good. Hence, no taxation of imputed rent and no deductions of any sort are applied. There is also no taxation of capital gains.

Some states provide loan guarantees for owner-occupied and rented residential buildings. There is however no general federal guarantee scheme for mortgage loans in place.

The "Eigenheimzulage" has been since its introduction in 1996, the centerpiece of the home ownership subsidy system in Germany. It took the place of the tax subsidization of homeownership via a manipulated investment good model applied before. The old funding model allowed for the deduction of depreciation and interest on mortgage debt from income tax. The imputed rental value was set deliberately too low, however. The criticism of the tax incentive model was directed particularly against its regressive distributional effect. This was also seen as a disadvantage for the relatively income poor East German households. In contrast, the allowances scheme newly introduced in 1996 was independent of the tax situation of subsidized households. The income limits were rather generous, especially for married couples.[32]

---

[32] With the Eigenheimzulage a tangible incentive for home ownership formation of broad layers of the population had been created. A family with two children initially received for a newly built residential property up to DM 64,000 grants over a period of 8 years. Despite the privilege of new construction projects a large effect on the number of residential completions was not to be observed. After the housing completions in 1- and 2-family buildings had increased by over 25 per cent between 1996 and 1999, since the turn of the millennium, they started to fall in a ten-year downward trend.

The Eigenheimzulage is not granted any longer since 1 January 2006. However, it has continued because of her eight-year eligibility period until 2013. The Eigenheimzulage was replaced by the promotion of homeownership as a form of private funded pension schemes (the so-called "Riester" pension). Apart from that, private homeownership is still supported by the following instruments:

- KfW Homeownership Program
- Social Housing
- Housing benefits for homeowners
- Urban development funding instruments
- Promotion of advance savings via a savings premium ("Wohnungsbauprämie")

The latter instruments with the exception of Wohnungsbauprämie and the KfW Homeownership Program do not focus exclusively on the promotion of homeownership, however. Thus, the housing allowance is also granted to tenants and social housing subsidies are also allocated to the construction of social rental housing. Even urban subsidies, such as the accelerated depreciation for listed buildings, are not reserved for owner-occupied housing.

To promote real estate investment, the public KfW bank offers a full range of loan and grant programs with different emphases: Homeownership, energy efficient construction and renovation, age-friendly conversion and housing modernization.

The social housing programs for the promotion of homeownership help the benefiting households by the granting of subsidized mortgage loans. However, access is limited by low income limits. In 2010 57.643 social housing units were subsidized, thereof 26.798 property measures (i.e. promotion of individual homeownership).[33]

---

[33] Social housing subsidies are either granted to investors for the creation of social rental dwellings or to needy individuals to help them to build a home of their own.

The advance savings promotion granted since several decades is marked by low income limits and a low subvention intensity.[34]

The funding of mortgage credit in Germany is bank-dominated and specialist banks, the Bausparkassen (equivalent to building societies) play a very important role. The Bauspar system is an established means of long-term equity capital formation for house purchase. Savers make regular contractual savings contributions over many years, and when the contract matures they receive not only the accumulated capital plus interest, but also a mortgage loan at a fixed rate. The use of Bausparen prior to buying a home is widespread in Germany and the savings contributions are publicly subsidized (see above).

Market penetration of the German Bauspar sector is very high.[35] The most important factors explaining the success of Bausparen in Germany are presumably the tight lending requirements for mortgage credit, especially in terms of LTV requirements (although the direction of the causation is not clear) and the long-term commitment of the government to subsidize this specific type of savings process. German households are used to waiting and saving more money instead of buying a home at an early stage of their life cycle. The average age of first-time buyers, at 40 years, is much higher in Germany than in many other countries.

---

[34] The advance savings promotion consists of two components, the housing bonus and employee savings bonus ("Wohnungsbauprämie" and "Arbeitnehmersparzulage"). Bauspar-savers can claim for the housing bonus on their savings up to a taxable annual income of € 25,600 per year for singles and € 51,200 for married couples. The premium is 8.8 % of the amounts yearly saved. However, only a maximum of savings of € 512.00 for singles or € 1,024.00 for married couples is subsidized, the maximum annual premium being € 90.11 or € 45.06, respectively. A premium of 9 percent (employee savings bonus) is granted on saving schemes, which are paid directly by the employer from the wages. The income limits are, however, significantly lower than for the housing bonus. The employee savings bonus is paid on deposits up to a maximum of 470 € per year.

[35] Every second German household has at least one Bauspar contract. There are about 26 million Bauspar savers with approximately 30 million accounts. This corresponds to a total contract sum of approximately € 763 billion Euro (around a third of German GDP or 3.5 times the volume of outstanding mortgage Pfandbriefe). 7 of 10 homebuyers / homebuilders use Bauspar savings funds (Verband der Privaten Bausparkassen 2012, p. 18).

The most important subsidy for homeowners is currently the "Riester pension". The creation of a voluntary funded pension in the form of financial assets, but also in the form of homeownership ("Wohn-Riester": "Residential Riester") is promoted with allowances or tax advantages.

In the financial assets variant monthly payments are made into a Riester certified savings product, so for example in a certified investment fund-related pension insurance. In this way pension assets are created, which are later converted into a pension based on actuarial principles. In the repayment phase however the Riester pension is subject in full to income tax ("deferred taxation").

Relating to the Wohn-Riester the government funding, refers to (Bauspar-) savings or principal payments under savings or loan contracts for the acquisition or construction of owner-occupied residential property or cooperative shares. It is however not permissible to use it for modernization, renovation, or repair of an existing home or for the restructuring of an existing mortgage loan.

The amount of the basic allowance is 154 euros per year.[36] To fully exploit it, Riester pension savers must save at least four per cent of their previous year's gross income (up to a maximum of 2,100 euros). Wohn-Riester savers have to make correspondingly high principal or savings payments.

The deferred taxation is regulated as follows for the Wohn-Riester: For the subsidized savings and principal payments a subsidy account in maintained. The accumulated capital is compounded by an interest rate of 2 percent annually. This results in a notional capital amount on which the saver must pay income tax when retiring. Hence if Wohn-Riester savers on average achieve an effective rate of return higher than 2 per cent (internal rate of return based on development of imputed rent, running costs and capital gains), there is a tax advantage for the Wohn-Riester savers.

Be that as it may, as compared with other countries, the current German housing subsidy system assures neutrality of tenures by and large. There is

[36] For married couples two separate loan agreements can be completed to allow both partners to benefit from the allowance. The child allowance is 185 euros per child per year. For children who are born in 2008 or later, a higher allowance of 300 euros is paid.

no clear bias towards homeownership. The "Eigenheimzulage" was cancelled in 2006 already. In personal income taxation the own house is treated as a consumption good. Currently, the most important subsidy is the Wohn-Riester and no capital gains taxation is applied in case of a sale of an owner-occupied home.

4.6 Housing allowances

Housing allowances ("Wohngeld"), are available in Germany irrespective of the status of the dwelling and the same rules apply for social and privately rented dwellings. The amount of Wohngeld a household is entitled to receive is determined by the number of family members in the household, the total annual family income, and the amount of rent or mortgage payment that qualifies for support. The scheme has income and rent ceilings, the levels of which depend on household size and local rent level.

People living on social assistance cannot claim Wohngeld but receive housing benefit (and help with their heating costs) as part of their income support benefit. For example, unemployed people with insufficient income get housing benefit as part of Arbeitslosengeld II (ALG II). It is not a complementary social security benefit like Wohngeld, but instead a last resort safety-net meant to ensure that people's basic living needs are met. Housing costs are fully covered, but only for what is deemed to be an "adequate" home. Adequacy is subject to size and rent ceilings that vary regionally.[37]

In 2011, 770 000 households were in receipt of Wohngeld (1.9 per cent of all households). The total expenditure for Wohngeld in that year was 1.5 billion Euros. The number of ALG II receiving households is much higher, however. In June 2013, 3,183,394 households (7.8 per cent of all households) were in receipt of housing benefit and heating cost support with their income support benefit (ALG II). The total cost for that kind of housing benefit will be around 14 billion Euros in the year 2013.

---

[37] Claimants whose flat is more expensive than the price ceilings need to try to trim down their housing costs, e.g. by moving into a cheaper flat or renting out a part of it (for details see Kofner 2007a).

4.7 Reforms effects on the housing market

The German PRS is a cornerstone of housing provision rather than a residual sector focused on the poor and those unable to buy their home. Private landlords serve a broad range of target groups. Moreover, there is much less "cultural fixation" on homeownership in Germany than in many Anglo-Saxon countries and private renting is not seen as an inferior tenure. The German PRS has always provided for a wide range of housing quality and hence German households do not need to become homeowners in order to access housing of the standard that they require.

Open-ended tenancies and very strong security of tenure ensure that private renting can provide long-term or even lifetime accommodation for German households. At the same time, asymmetric contracts give renters who wish to move home the freedom to do so. Second generation type rent regulation means that tenants are not exposed to sharp, short-term increases in rents even in tight housing markets. All of these factors have helped to maintain demand for private renting relative to homeownership among many moderate and well-off households.

In terms of accessibility and affordability the performance of the German PRS is mixed. The German housing market is characterized by a number of urban hot spots with extremely low vacancy rates and rent levels far above average. Places like Hamburg, Munich and Frankfurt[38] are focal points of housing need since many years.

In general, residential letting is not an unattractive business for landlords. The tax system treats rental housing as an investment and hence provides for depreciation allowances, mortgage interest tax relief, deduction of maintenance costs and negative gearing. The fact that capital gains are exempt from tax if the property is held for at least ten years, helps to encourage long-term investment in rental property. However, after-tax rental yields have been suppressed since the abolition of accelerated depreciation on new housing investment in 2006.

---

[38] With vacancy rates of 0.7, 0.6 and 1.0 per cent at year end 2011, respectively according to Techem-empirica-Leerstandsindex

The attractions of German residential real estate as a long-term, secure investment are reflected by the financial investor's ability to re-finance and sell all or parts of their portfolios to other investors. Indeed, the German PRS has become a sought after safe haven investment for international and domestic capital in the wake of the Global Financial Crisis (GFC).

In terms of its contribution to labor market flexibility the performance of the German PRS is improvable. This is due to the effects of rental price laws which tend to create split markets in excess demand situations.

5 Barriers to a well-functioning housing market and PRS

5.1 Supply side barriers

The prospects for the German PRS are surely not hampered by all-too-generous subsidies for other housing tenures (social housing, public housing, homeownership). All in all, the current German housing subsidy system does not discriminate the PRS.

Planning may have supply-restraining effects in certain regions. The planning authority lies with the municipalities. The incentive system for the zoning of new residential areas could be insufficient. This is also a question of tax distribution in the system of financial equalization. In many cities, there are considerable reservations about high-rise buildings. High-rise residential developments if greenfield or brownfield do not seem to be welcome in general. Cities such as Munich, Hamburg or Cologne have specific design principles that serve the preservation and protection of the "City Crown".

There are no obvious barriers to institutional investment in PRS dwellings. However, it occurs only rarely. Open-end property funds usually tend to neglect residential buildings. Close-end property funds concentrate on certain niches of the residential segment, e.g. monuments and student dwellings. Insurances and pension funds usually have a very low share of real estate in their portfolios. On average it is far below the legal maximum share, the effective share being around 5 per cent.[39] German REITs are not allowed to invest in existing residential buildings (Kofner 2007b). Foreign Private Equity Funds on the other hand have closed a lot of important package deals in the years before the GFC. Nowadays the public opinion relating to takeovers of public housing companies by Private Equity Funds is hostile. Also, they have turned to other investment targets. Recently, the housing portfolios of South German Landesbanken were sold to

---

[39] According to § 3 Abs. 5 Anlageverordnung max. 25 per cent real estate share of the total portfolio is allowed for life insurances and pension funds

consortiums of German institutional investors. Those investors seem to have changed their minds about residential real estate investments.

The performance record of the German capital market in terms of allocating equity funds to residential investment is surely poor. This is evidenced by the small number of listed housing stocks (for the most part a result of the exit of Private Equity Funds via IPOs). Capital market legislation should try to reform existing investment vehicles or create new ones in order to make indirect residential investment more accessible and attractive especially for small investors. This is suggested by the greater efficiency of indirect investments in real estate: The portfolio can be handled quicker, with much lower transaction costs and much less exposure to accumulation risks. Here it might be advisable to combine tax privileges of investment vehicles with certain rules of conduct, so that a measurable contribution is made to social return.

5.2   Appropriateness of yields in the PRS

The returns that can be obtained from the long-term lease of privately financed housing, are generally within in a range from 3.5 to 6.5 percent (excluding capital gains) for professional landlords. According to the housing industry association GdW the rates of return on equity capital range between 0.5 (small organizations in East Germany) and 7 per cent (large organizations in West Germany) among limited liability member organizations (average: 4.4 per cent, see GdW 2013, pp. 86-89). The GdW returns on total capital scatter much less around an average of 3.3 per cent. Yields obtained by professional private landlords are not likely to fall behind. However, the average return on total capital employed in the German SME is around 10 per cent.

The regulation of rents has a dampening effect on return expectations and more specifically in the short to medium term. In tight housing markets, the system can also bring along a price-capping effect in the long run under certain circumstances.

The Net Cold Rent (NCR) multipliers[40] have generally risen recently. They have risen sharply at certain focal points of housing needs. In Hamburg,

Munich and other places buyers often pay multipliers significantly higher than 20.

Since the abolition of the cost recovery rent ("Kostenmiete") the returns of the landlords in social housing are not uniformly regulated any longer (then 4 per cent return on equity). Nowadays the return expectations result from the program conditions (subsidy benefit, special rent ceilings) and the cost efficiency of the investor. The subsidization of social housing currently has the problem that – given the extremely low interest-rate environment – not a sufficient number of investors can be attracted, so that not always the targeted number of social dwellings can be built (for example, Düsseldorf).

5.3   Subsidization of social housing

The subsidies for social housing have been very extensive in the past and they have acted as an important factor in building up the large rental housing stock in Germany. In the 50s and 60s social housing has made a decisive contribution to the elimination of the war-related housing shortage. Of the nearly 7 million dwellings finished in the period 1950-1962 no less than 61 per cent were social housing (1950-1956: 69.4 per cent of all housing completions.)

The importance of government intervention for the housing market in the years of reconstruction can also be demonstrated by considering the sources of funding for housing investment. Between 1950 and 1962, 27.7 percent of housing investment was financed from public funds.

Later the social housing programs were focused on specific target groups and their share in total completions fell permanently. Between 2002 and 2010 an average of about 65,000 social dwellings was subsidized including for the greater part measures in the existing housing stock. The overall number of social units has declined in those eight years by one-third, to less than 1.7 million by the end of 2010[41]. Since 2008 the number of newly built

---

[40] The Net Cold Rent Multiplier is the ratio of the price of a real estate investment to its annual rental income before extra costs and expenses (e.g. administration and maintenance costs).

[41] Antwort des Staatssekretärs im Bundesministerium für Verkehr, Bau und

social rental dwellings stagnated between 10,000 and 12,000 units per year (Pestel-Institut 2013, p. 2).

The development of social-housing legislation was characterized by increasing flexibility and regionalization (Eichener 2005, p 1). States were granted ever more control over the design of the programs (determining for example eligibility requirements and maximum rent).

Currently, social housing is characterized by short lock-in periods, rents at the bottom end of the LRR, an income orientation of the subsidization, a small-scale distribution of completions, including mixing with privately financed dwellings and a preference for creating social dwellings in the existing housing stock.

The federal financial assistance to the states for social housing purposes is limited until 2019 to € 518.2 million per year. The subsidy from the federal government is distributed pro rata to population. Hence, the different need for social housing is not taken into account in any way. City-states with tight housing markets are not subsidized more intensely than area states with large housing surpluses. As part of a federal mixed financing the federal government does not seem to be able to distribute the funds according to local needs.

The states supplement these federal funds, but with completely different multipliers between 0 and 10.[42] As of 2020, there will be no more compensation payments from the federal government.

With a share of only 4 per cent of the total housing stock, the German social housing sector is currently smaller than in many comparable

Stadtentwicklung, Jan Mücke (FDP), auf die parlamentarische Anfrage der Abgeordneten Caren Lay.

[42] Some states do not promote social housing at all, but rather use the funds for other permissible uses (e.g. modernization or urban development). As of 2014, even those generously defined use restrictions will not be applicable any longer. In contrast, Hamburg subsidizes social housing with a multiplier of 10:1, i.e. one federal Euro is supplemented with 10 euros from the state budget. Berlin, Brandenburg, Bremen, Mecklenburg-Vorpommern, Saarland and Saxony in 2010 have no longer supported the development of new social dwellings. North Rhine-Westphalia is with 5397 new social rental housing units for lower-income strata at the top of the statistics, followed by Hamburg (2253) and Bavaria (1617). Source: Bild-Zeitung from 27. November 2012. Completions per capita were highest in Hamburg.

countries. It has contributed to the growth of the private rental sector in the past however, either by the expiry of the social status of the dwellings after the subsidized credits have been paid back or by the sale of whole housing companies to the private sector (Voigtländer, 2006, pp. 12-13).[43] Public or factory-related housing companies were sold especially to financial investors. However, these actors in the PRS still provide affordable housing and no exchange of target groups on a large scale has taken place until today.

The main effect of the diminishing of social housing subsidies was a permanent shrinkage in the total number of social dwellings. The decline of completion numbers started in the 70s already. Since a long time the number of dwellings losing their social status – all social housing subsidies in Germany are temporary by their very nature – each year outnumbers by far the number of newly constructed or otherwise created social dwellings.

As was said before Germany does not have "social landlords". Social dwellings are owned by public and private landlords as well. The public landlords are usually limited companies. That means they can go bankrupt without the lenders being able to take recourse on the public owner. There may be an implicit guarantee, however. On the other hand, the public landlords do not receive any specific supply side subsidies. Land cost rebates are presumably granted sometimes on a case-specific basis.

Public and private landlords, if they own any social dwellings or not, are free to engage in any type of commercial investment (e.g. privately financed residential development, commercial or infrastructure development, electricity or heat production) and there are no limits on cross-subsidization in whatever direction (remember that subsidies for social housing are strictly project-bound). In fact, investors should make a profit from social housing development, albeit to a limited extent. The profit margin is an

---

[43] In Germany, the status of a social dwelling is not permanent. Regardless of whether a private or a public investor has built a social dwelling using public subsidies, the dwelling loses its social legal status, once the public development loans are fully repaid. But that does not rule out that the former social dwelling is still in public ownership. On the other hand, social dwellings can be sold to private investors before the end of the social commitments.

implicit part of the contract between the landlord and the municipality that provides the social housing subsidy.

Also, the public owners frequently use their public housing companies as promoters for infrastructure or brownfield development projects.

In Germany, the social housing sector causes only limited distortion of competition. It is well integrated in most respects with the private sector. The dualism between the two sectors is limited to the necessary minimum.

5.4 Lock-in effects/barriers for mobility of social tenants

A lock-in effect is almost inevitable in social housing. Especially long-term social tenants benefit from low rents. Also, due to income increases or reductions in the number of family members, many households have grown out of the legal income limits.

In most states, a "compensation" is levied to compensate for the rent advantages of the social tenants with too high income (§ § 34-37 Wohnraumförderungsgesetz). However, only part of their rent advantages is skimmed off. The income burden of housing costs is very different from state to state. Only about 60 per cent of the ones profiting from undue rent advantages are forced to make compensation payments. Generally speaking all households who profit from undue rent advantages have a reduced incentive to move to another city for professional reasons. It is however questionable if rent advantages should be skimmed off always and everywhere. Sometimes it may be desirable to stabilize an already deteriorating social mix in a large settlement.

The mobility effects of the social housing system also depend on the local supply situation relating to social housing. Against the background of a general shortage of social housing[44], considerable barriers to mobility may

---

[44] A recent study of Pestel Institute concludes that currently some 4 million social dwellings are lacking in Germany. Only one in five cash-strapped households currently has any chance to get a social dwelling. The Pestel Institute calculated a current national need of about 5.6 million social dwellings. Currently, however, only 1.6 million are available in the housing market. See Pestel-Institut 2012, p. 9.

result. Especially in the boomtowns and hot spots of housing scarcity the PRS does not provide an affordable alternative.

A social tenant from Hamburg, also has the right to a social dwelling in Cologne. There are long waiting lists in both cities, however. Hence, the incentive to move from Hamburg to Cologne or the other way round in order to get a better-paid job or a job at all is reduced for social tenants. Even in the very improbable case that they immediately get a new social dwelling, the rent may be higher. This will certainly be the case if they have to supply themselves in the general housing market or PRS. The difference will only partly be covered by a higher claim for housing allowances.

However, the social housing sector with 1.6 million dwellings left and accounting only for about 4 per cent of the total housing stock is probably not the greatest obstacle to labor market mobility in Germany. More significant barriers to mobility are likely created by the general rental laws (see above, 4.2.7).

5.5 Flexibility of conversion from other tenures

The conversion of social housing to general rental housing is inevitable. As soon as the investor has paid back his public mortgage loan the dwelling loses its social status, i.e. from then on it will be free of special rent regulation and the occupancy commitment. General rental laws will be applicable and the dwelling can be let to any tenant independent of his income. In case the investor has received public grants the social status lasts for another three years after the end of the grant period. Since the 90s there has been a noticeable reduction in the commitment periods. They now predominantly range between 10 and 15 years, whilst in classical social housing commitment periods between 45 and 50 years were common.

In case of early full repayment of the public mortgage loan the "social" status ends ten years after the public funds were paid back, but no later than the end of the normal repayment period (§ 16 para 1 Wohnungsbindungsgesetz).

If one wants to keep the number of social dwellings constant, such a system requires permanent activity to replace the social dwellings that have been switched their status to privately financed. Since a large part of the social dwellings is still owned by public housing organizations, an important part of the dwellings switched does not become part of the PRS, however. On the other hand there are no legal obstacles to the sale of social dwellings to the private sector.

Social rental dwellings can be converted to condominiums. In this case, the buyer of the converted social dwelling cannot terminate the lease as long as the social status lasts (dependent on the loan conditions, see above).

Social rental dwellings have never been turned into owner-occupied dwellings during the commitment period to the knowledge of the author. Only public dwellings in Eastern Germany were sold to their tenants with some rebate, but that project was not very successful anyway.

There are no legal barriers for (temporarily) converting owner-occupied housing to PRS housing. The owner can rent out his house or condominium any time. Doing so has important consequences for personal income tax. Rent income is taxable, but the running costs can be deducted. Converting back is more difficult because even the tenant of a single family home or a condominium profits from general dismissal protection.

In Germany there is no distinctive mortgage market segment for buy-to-let-mortgages. Neither the interest rates are systematically higher, nor are the LTV requirements. The loan conditions for rented multi-family buildings depend on the characteristics of the individual property and the amount of the loan. So-called "Tableau conditions" such as, for example, in private home finance are not available. However, the conditions for the financing of multi-family houses closely depend on the conditions for owner-occupied housing. Lenders obviously believe that both types of mortgages have a comparable default risk.

6 Sources

Arbeitsgemeinschaft für zeitgemäßes Bauen e.V. (ARGE//eV, 2013): Kostensteigernde Effekte im Wohnungsbau, Bauforschungsbericht Nr. 65.

BBSR [Federal Office on Building, Urban Affairs and Spatial Development] (2012): Housing and Property Markets in Germany in 2011 at a Glance, Bonn: Federal Office on Building, Urban Affairs and Spatial Development.

BMVBS [Bundesministerium für Verkehr, Bau und Stadtentwicklung] (2012): Wohnen und Bauen in Zahlen 2011/2012, 7. Auflage, Stand: Juni 2012.

Bundesministerium für Verkehr, Bau- und Wohnungswesen (2004): Nachhaltige Stadtentwicklung – ein Gemeinschaftswerk. Städtebaulicher Bericht der Bundesregierung 2004.

Department of Environment, United Kingdom: Housing Policy: Technical Volume (London, HMSO, 1977), Part III.

DIW (2013): SOEPmonitor 1984-2011: Time Series on housing related indicators in Germany, Berlin.

Eichener, V. (2005): Zukünftige Schwerpunkte der Wohnungspolitik ... aus Sicht der Wissenschaft, erschienen in: Wohnungspolitik vor der Neujustierung. 40. Königsteiner Gespräch, 7./8. April 2005, Schriftenreihe des Instituts für Städtebau, Wohnungswirtschaft und Bausparwesen, Bd. 67, Berlin: domus 2005, S. 59-69.

Flagge, I. (ed., 1995): Geschichte des Wohnens, Band 5: Von 1945 bis heute. Aufbau, Neubau, Umbau, Deutsche Verlags-Anstalt (DVA), Stuttgart.

GdW (2013): Wohnungswirtschaftliche Daten und Trends 2013/2014: Zahlen und Analysen aus der Jahresstatistik des GdW, Berlin, November 2013.

Howenstine, J. (1981): Private rental housing abroad: dwindling supply stirs concern, in: Monthly Labor Review, September 1981, vol. 104, No. 9, S. 38-42.

IWU Institut Wohnen und Umwelt GmbH (2005): Auswirkungen des Wegfalls von Sozialbindungen und des Verkaufs öffentlicher Wohnungsbestände auf die Wohnungsversorgung unterstützungsbedürftiger Haushalte, Teilabschlussbericht im Rahmen des vom BMBF geförderten Forschungsverbundes „Wohnungslosigkeit und Hilfen in Wohnungsnotfällen", Darmstadt.

Kämper, O. (1938): Wohnungswirtschaft und Grundkredit, de Gruyter.

Kletečka, A. / Oberhammer, P. / Wall, A. (ed., 2011): Soziales Mietrecht In Europa, Springer.

Koalitionsvertrag (2013): Koalitionsvertrag zwischen CDU, CSU und SPD: Deutschlands Zukunft gestalten, 18. Legislaturperiode.

Kofner, S. (2003): Die Formation der deutschen Wohnungspolitik nach dem Zweiten Weltkrieg, Teil I-III, in: Deutsche Wohnungswirtschaft, 55. Jg. (2003), Heft 10-12.

Kofner, S. (2006), 'Private Equity investment in housing: the case of Germany', paper for the European Network of Housing Research (ENHR) International Housing Conference, Ljubljana, Slovenia, 2 - 5 July.

Kofner, S. (2007a): Housing Allowances in Germany, in: Kemp. P. (ed., 2007): Housing Allowances in Comparative Perspective, The Policy Press, S. 159-192.

Kofner, S. (2007b): Wohnimmobilien als Investitionsobjekte der deutschen REITs, in: Wohnungswirtschaft und Mietrecht, 60. Jg. (2007), Heft 4, S. 183-185.

Kofner, S. (2009): Private Vermieter, in: Wohnungswirtschaft und Mietrecht, 62. Jg., Heft 3.

Pestel-Institut (2012): Bedarf an Sozialwohnungen in Deutschland, Untersuchung im Auftrag der Wohnungsbau-Initiative, Hannover.

Pestel-Institut (2013): Analyse zum Wohnungsbau in Deutschland: Kernforderungen und Fakten, Hannover, Oktober 2013.

Sachverständigenrat für die Begutachtung der gesamtwirtschaftlichen Entwicklung (SVR 2013): Jahresgutachten 2013/14 „Gegen eine rückwärtsgewandte Wirtschaftspolitik", veröffentlicht am 13.11.2013.

Statistisches Bundesamt (2000): 50 Jahre Wohnen in Deutschland, Stuttgart: Metzler-Poeschel.

Statistisches Bundesamt (2013a): zensus 2011: Gebäude und Wohnungen, Ergebnisse zum Stand Mai 2013.

Statistisches Bundesamt (2013b): Statistisches Jahrbuch 2013: Kapitel 5: Wohnen.

TRAWOS [Institut für Transformation, Wohnen und Soziale Raumentwicklung] (2012): Aktuelle Geschäftsmodelle von Finanzinvestoren im Themenfeld Wohnungswirtschaftlicher Wandel und neue Finanzinvestoren, Gutachten im Auftrag der Enquètekommission Wohnungswirtschaftlicher Wandel und Neue Finanzinvestoren auf den Wohnungsmärkten in NRW, Görlitz: TRAWOS, Hochschule Zittau/Görlitz.

Verband der Privaten Bausparkassen (ed. 2012): Bausparen in Deutschland.

Voigtländer, M. (2006): Mietwohnungsmarkt und Wohneigentum: Zwei Seiten einer Medaille, Gutachten für den Verband deutscher Pfandbriefbanken.

Woebken-Ekert (2005): Bausparen: Die letzte Bastion, in: Die Zeit Nr. 35 v. 25.08.2005.

7 Annex: Homeownership rates in Germany

	According to age of principal earner		
	Total number of households (1,000)	Homeowner households (1,000)	Per cent
below 25	1,799	128	7.1
25-30	2,658	288	10.8
30-40	5,718	1,691	29.6
40-50	8,111	3,873	47.7
50-60	6,704	3,616	53.9
60-65	2,575	1,435	55.7
65 and older	10,891	5,968	54.8
	According to household size		
	Total number of households (1,000)	Homeowner households (1,000)	Per cent
1 person	15,281	4,234	27.7
2 persons	13,304	6,903	51.9
3 persons	4,873	2,665	54.7
4 persons	3,678	2,379	64.7
5 and more persons	1,321	817	61.8

	According to monthly household income (EUR)		
	Total number of households (1,000)	Homeowner households (1,000)	Per cent
below 900	4,504	736	16.3
900-1300	5,502	1,514	27.5
1300-1500	2,885	937	32.5
1500-2000	6,028	2,333	38.7
2000-3200	9,429	4,844	51.4
3200-4500	4,463	2,954	66.2
4500-6000	1,788	1,324	74.0
6000-7500	542	422	77.9
7500 and more	519	402	77.5

	According to social position		
	Total number of households (1,000)	Homeowner households (1,000)	Per cent
Self-employed	2,902	1,681	57.9
Employed	23,145	10,145	43.8
Unemployed	1,474	182	12.4
Inactive	13,837	6,670	48.2

Table: Homeownership rate in Germany

Source: Statistisches Bundesamt, Zusatzerhebung zum Mikrozensus 2010